Grateful
Every day

STORIES TO OPEN YOUR HEART
TO THE BLESSINGS OF LIFE

VISIONARY DR. RENEE SUNDAY

© Sunday Publishing Company
Reneesunday.com

Table of Contents

ABOUT DR. RENEE SUNDAY

From poverty to purpose, Dr. Renee Sunday created a stellar career. Empowering and educating, this ordained minister serves in media, business development, and healthcare. As a Board-Certified Anesthesiologist for nineteen years, she's been voted as one of the top 100 in the nation.

GRATEFUL EVERYDAY

This "platform builder" founded Renee Sunday Enterprises and Sunday Publishing Company. She teaches others to "Be Seen, Be Heard & Get Paid." Between media, consulting, coaching, and speaking, this best-selling author freely shares love and support instilled early on.

Gracing platforms alongside Oprah, T.D. Jakes, Paula White, and Jekalyn Carr, Dr. Sunday continues to transform lives.

Grateful - a sense of thankfulness, loving and appreciating life, a person or an experience.

I'm truly grateful for God's blessing upon me and my family everyday with His abundant mercies and Grace. Words can't express my love, honor and devotion to Him. My parents who instilled the habit of Gratitude in me at an early age, gave me the ability to always give and help others.

GRATEFUL EVERYDAY

This also sparked my potentials to help others identify their purpose in life and build a platform to Be Seen, Heard and Get Paid. My journey of gratitude everyday opens many opportunities which has and will continue to offer me the passion to bless everyone I come in contact with.

My motto: If I can help someone as I travel through life's journey, then my living will not be in vain. Having a grateful heart invites miracles, overflowing experiences, opportunities and finally, it makes dreams come to pass.

GRATEFUL EVERYDAY

2 CORINTHIANS 4:15

All this is for your benefit,
so that the grace that is reaching
more and more people may cause
thanksgiving to overflow to the glory of God.

ELIZABETH PETER OKORO

ELIZABETH PETER OKORO

an editor and proofreader, a wife and mother of two beautiful children. She has joined several research companies and NGO's to help find solutions to female genital mutilation in Africa. She has also participated in several projects which were initiated to fight polio and malaria in Africa.

GRATEFUL EVERYDAY

What being grateful means to me is showing appreciation and gratitude for the good things around me, my family, my children, and so on. Being grateful for what God has done and is still doing in my life, for the air I breathe in and out, for my shelter, for the food I eat, and most importantly, the good health that He has given me.

I'm grateful for my wonderful husband and children, who stand and also comfort me when I'm down. I'm really grateful that I have found God's love in my heart, and it brightens my day.

Gratitude cleanses the soul, and it makes you feel alive. Being grateful, no matter the situation or circumstances, is what we should learn as humans, because there are others who encounter worst problems than what you think you are currently passing through. Psalm 7:17 should always be our affirmation.

GRATEFUL EVERYDAY

1 THESSALONIANS 5:16-18 | KJV

Rejoice evermore.
Pray without ceasing.
In every thing give thanks:
for this is the will of God in Christ
Jesus concerning you.

YVONA PAYNE

ABOUT YVONA PAYNE

CEO and Founder of Savvy Sexy Sheek Fashion, a Plus and Regular Size Clothing and Accessories Boutique (www.savvysexysheek.com). She is a Motivational Speaker, Business and Boutique Start Up Coach who shares her challenges; which help encourage herself and others with their present and future success.

GRATEFUL EVERYDAY

Grateful to me is being thankful for all things, especially waking up alive, well, able to use my own limbs, being of sound mind, body and soul. Also, having a clear conscience and a thankful heart.

"LIFE" and the opportunity to make a change in my life and the lives of others, especially my immediate family and in my business.

Gratitude "being Thankful" helps you grow and expand, especially if you use gratitude to make sense of your past, let it brings joy and laughter into your present life and those around you and creates a vision for your future. With God, Faith, Praise and Patience you can accomplish more than you can ever imagine.

GRATEFUL EVERYDAY

Philippians 4:6-7 | KJV

Be careful for nothing;
but in every thing by prayer and
supplication with thanksgiving let your
requests be made known unto God. And the
peace of God, which passeth all understanding,
shall keep your hearts and minds
through Christ Jesus.

BRENDA SAWYER

ABOUT BRENDA SAWYER

Brenda Sawyer was born and raised in New York City and currently resides in Philadelphia. Her strong spiritual foundation acknowledges that she is a true Christian who believes that she can do all things through Christ who strengthens her. As a young child, Brenda has always had a passion for teaching and imparting knowledge in the society and world at large. After graduating from Hunter College with a dual major in Psychology and Early Childhood Education, Brenda taught elementary school for twenty-six years in a School District of Philadelphia. Brenda holds a second Master's degree from Cabrini College. In addition to being a published author of Encouraging Words For The Mind, Spirit and Soul, she is also the Founder and CEO of GIRLS WALKING WITH INTEGRITY EMPOWERING FOR DESTINY (GWWI), a Christian mentoring ministry which empowers young ladies between the ages of 8-18 to trust in God, believe in their dreams and all that God has called them to be.

GRATEFUL EVERYDAY

Being grateful means that I have the "Spirit of the Living God" living on the inside of me, allowing me to live, move and have my being in Him alone.

I am grateful that God allows me to wake up, clothed in my right mind with the use and activities of my limbs. He allows me to have a second chance to live my life to the fullest.

So, wake up decreeing and declaring over your life, "This is the day which the LORD has made I will rejoice and be glad in it. " Psalm 118:24

GRATEFUL EVERYDAY

1 Corinthians 15:57 | KJV

But thanks
be to God, which giveth
us the victory through our
Lord Jesus Christ.

CHRISTIANA J. WILLIAMS

ABOUT CHRISTIANA J. WILLIAMS

Christiana J. Williams is pursuing a Master's degree at the University of Alabama at Birmingham. She is a member of TESOL and Phi Kappa Phi. She graduated with a Bachelor of Arts degree from UAB cum laude and with distinguished honors. She looks forward to pursuing a career in teaching

GRATEFUL EVERYDAY

Being grateful everyday means that I am contented with and thankful for what I have. It means thanking God for everything that He has already done and for what He is doing right now. It means being grateful for both the good and bad things that happen in life because they help mold people into who they are. Being grateful means focusing on the positive things in life. When a person is grateful, they feel better mentally, spiritually and emotionally. Everyone has something to be grateful for. When a person is grateful, they view and respond to events that occur in life more positively. Gratefulness helps people

cope with difficult situations better. When people encounter a grateful person, they are inspired to become a grateful person as well.

GRATEFUL EVERYDAY

I am grateful for the uncountable things God has done and still doing. First and foremost, I am grateful that God has allowed me to see another bright day and to be in good health. I am thankful that I have access to food, clothing and shelter.

I am grateful for my family and friends. I am indebted to my role models, who have taught me how to carry myself as a woman. It is a blessing to live in a country that is safe, clean and prosperous. I am thankful that I have the opportunity to pursue a career that I am passionate about. It is a blessing to be able to help other people reach or achieve their goals in life.

I have chosen the following quotes because they embody the essence of gratefulness.

- No matter what's happening, choose to be happy. Don't focus on what's wrong. Find something positive in your life. Thank God for the small things. Joel Osteen
- 1 Thessalonians 5:18 New International Version (NIV)
  Give thanks in all circumstances; for this is God's will for you in Christ Jesus.
- **1 Chronicles 16:34**
  Give thanks to the LORD, for he is good; his love endures forever.
- **Psalm 100:4**
  Enter his gates with thanksgiving and his courts with praise;
  give thanks to him and praise his name.

References

Bible Gateway. (2011). *Holy Bible, New International Version*. Retrieved from
https://www.biblegateway.com/passage/?search=1%20Chronicles+16&version=NIV

Lagacé, Maxime. (2019). *260 gratitude quotes that will double your happiness.* Retrieved from

https://wisdomquotes.com/gratitude-quotes/

Miller, J. (2016, July 8). *8 ways to have more gratitude every day.* Retrieved from https://www.forbes.com/sites/womensmedia/2016/07/08/8-ways-to-have-more-gratitude-every-day/#4e9912c01d54

GRATEFUL EVERYDAY

2 Thessalonians 1:3 | KJV

We are bound to thank God always
for you, brethren, as it is meet, because
that your faith groweth exceedingly,
and the charity of every one of
you all toward each other aboundeth.

PASTOR DORIS SMITH

ABOUT PASTOR DORIS SMITH

Pastor Doris Smith; retired after 29 years in Government Service.

Native Floridian, Teacher, Author (Collaborative Project) "**The Voice of Hope,**" Certified Professional Speaker; Life/Inspirational Coach, Host of **The Power Hour Line of Inspiration & Motivation,** Co-Host of **Facing Your Fears Radio Talk Show; wife and caregiver.**

GRATEFUL EVERYDAY

Being grateful everyday to me; means never taking life for granted; live it; love it and forgive in it. For it's only for a season; make it a great one — a life that will continue to speak positive and powerful things when your silent.

Truly grateful for everyday; that the Lord allows me the blessing; to breath, live and embrace every challenge as an opportunity to soar; humbly enough to always reach out to genuinely assist someone else in times of trouble and pain.

Pray Always; Rejoice Always; and Always give Thanks, in All Things; and nothing will hold you captive.
1 Thessalonians 5:16-18

GRATEFUL EVERYDAY

1 Chronicles 16:34 | KJV

O give thanks unto the Lord;
for he is good; for his mercy endureth for ever.

K ASHLEY

ABOUT K ASHLEY

K. Ashley is from Louisiana but currently resides in Atlanta, Georgia. She is a woman of God, mother, Nana to Zion and Gideon, sister, friend, mentor, and an educator by profession. She is passionate about traveling, crafting, and creating memories. Her life mission is to Educate, Empower, and Entertain.

GRATEFUL EVERYDAY

Being grateful is all about taking time to appreciate things. We must be grateful for sunny and rainy days. I am grateful that God is always there to save us from difficult situations.

I am grateful that I have a mouth to smile, voice to praise, worship and speak my truth. I am also grateful for having a tongue to speak life into people's lives and also taste good food.

Find something to be grateful for everyday no matter the circumstances, because God is in control in all seasons of your life.
Let your light shine during the growing season because eventually the harvest season will come!

GRATEFUL EVERYDAY

Psalm 9:1 | KJV

I will praise thee, O Lord, with my whole heart;
I will shew forth all thy marvellous works.

PASTOR IRENE FULMORE

ABOUT PASTOR IRENE FULMORE

Apostle Irene Fulmore is married to her wonderful husband Sandy Fulmore for 29 years. They have two adult children and three grandchildren. I am a full-time pastor along with our loving care outreach. We started our ministry on September 18, 2011, Christ the King Deliverance Ministry in Timmonsville, South Carolina.

GRATEFUL EVERYDAY

I am grateful to God for all that He has done and still doing. I'm truly blessed with a hard-working man of God and husband – Elder Sandy Fulmore who makes it easy for me to focus on the ministry without worrying about the household budget. We've been married for 29 years as of October 6, 2019, and we are blessed with two adult children, one daughter in law and three grandchildren. My son and his wife serve as youth pastors in the church and my daughter serves as the church administrator.

My two grandsons serve in the music ministry and my granddaughter is also a part of the youth ministry. My husband and I are also grateful for pastoring our church ministry. We thank God for the 8 years and we are grateful and honored to have a blessed church, family, and faithful ministry staff. I am so grateful to have safe drinking water. Grateful to be a blessing in our community, to give back school supplies, food, and clothes to families in need. I am grateful to have good health and healthy meal choices.

GRATEFUL EVERYDAY

I want to encourage everyone to be thankful and grateful because you are truly a blessing. Stay focused on God and don't allow your mind to be worried, stressed with people problems, and family issues. "With Jesus Christ in your life every day you're growing deeper in your faith no matter what you facing. You can find hope in God's word in the midst of what you're passing through. Take a moment to meditate on God's word." 1 Corinthians 15:57, be encouraged to give thanks and express your gratitude even when you may feel overwhelmed by the things you have to do that you simply forget to stop and reflect on why you should be grateful. But thanks be to God which giveth us the victory through our Lord Jesus Christ.

GRATEFUL EVERYDAY

Romans 11:36 | KJV

For of him, and through him, and to him,
are all things: to whom be glory for ever. Amen.

ZONDRA TATE

ABOUT ZONDRA TATE

As a resilient woman, Zondra Tate loves God and loves sharing her testimony. She's not only surviving for herself, but for her 3 children and 4 grandchildren, as well as the man who God sent to love her properly – Mr. Kenneth Tate. She is the owner of Heart Smile Motivation, LLC and believes that her life's journey will invoke others to be strong, keep the faith, and never give up!

GRATEFUL EVERYDAY

He Heard My Cry – He'll Hear Yours Too

You have an amazing gift of illumination. Yes, you can shine and shine brightly. And that is something to be proud of, because your light is proof that you are important. For that, you should be grateful. I know I am! Each and everyday, through the grace of God, I have peace of mind and joy that is unshakeable. I have control over my thoughts and emotions. And I admit that it's a blessing to choose happiness. But there was a time when I didn't feel that way.

Many won't admit it but depression is real, and it was very real in my life. From childhood and bleeding over into adulthood, God had to come and rescue me from myself. He is the only One who I can accredit for delivering me from depression. But I had to make a decision to get "tired of being sick and tired." I was in a bad place; I felt lost, unappreciated, and unworthy of love and attention. But there is such a freedom and peace that comes

GRATEFUL EVERYDAY

when you get your mind right – and this goes beyond what others may say or feel. I was so hard on myself at times and the thoughts I was having were simply unacceptable. But God!

My parents divorced when I was three years old. My mother remarried and my stepfather adopted us by giving us his last name. This was devastating to me because I thought it meant that my biological father no longer loved me. That was the first major self-worth downer that I can recall. In later years, I was exposed to molestation by babysitters, my stepfather, and an uncle. At age 14, I was raped; this resulted in the stillbirth of identical twin daughters that I was carrying. As you can imagine, this was a lot to deal with during my teen years. I then went into a deeper level of depression that caused me to become very promiscuous, believing that sexual activity would be my drug and take the pain away. Obviously, it didn't and things only got worse. I experienced one abusive and toxic relationship after another.

I became a single mother of three. Undoubtedly, I loved my children; however, it was often hard to be strong for them because I was struggling just to provide and survive. I tried alcohol, pain pills, and marijuana to compensate for the depression. Of course, it only made me feel worse. I became a grandmother at the age of 39 and that precious baby girl brought so much happiness. However, the void was still present. Nothing worldly healed my hurt. Then one day, at the age of 41, my faith was revived after hearing a Word from my Pastor, Apostle Stephen A. Davis. I totally surrendered and cried out to God. And even in the midst of my mess, He heard my cry – even through the uncontrollable tears. When I thought I was worthless and no one cared about me, He did. Daily, I express gratitude for being free in my mind and my emotions. Does this mean that I've not had any tests to challenge my mind? No! But I'm grateful everyday knowing that, through Him, healing and wholeness are possible! No matter what you have been through, know that you can have joy and love yourself – regardless of your past. He heard my cry and He'll hear yours too!

GRATEFUL EVERYDAY

Colossians 3:17 | KJV

And whatsoever ye do in word or deed,
do all in the name of the Lord Jesus, giving thanks
to God and the Father by him.

TOSHA TURNER

ABOUT TOSHA TURNER

Tosha is an accomplished motivational speaker and mentor. She believes in motivating women to be their best no matter where they are in life or the condition they find themselves. Her passion is for families to stick together and create healthy relationships. She is a native of Birmingham, Alabama, and a graduate of Ramsay High School. She is presently furthering her education in the field of Business and Human Resources. She is married, has one daughter and three grandchildren. Her hobbies are reading, writing and traveling. She is a member of the Universalist Unitarian Church of Homewood.

GRATEFUL EVERYDAY

Starting my day with gratitude immediately shifts my thought process to an area of positivity. It causes my outlook for the day to be full of hope and I feel like I can soar high to accomplish things I otherwise would think impossible. The realization that I have another opportunity to begin again with a clean slate and affect the people that I come in contact with that day in a peaceful, caring, uplifting way allows room for me to receive and hear what the universe has for me. When I take the time to actually look around me and see what's right in my life instead of focusing on what's wrong, the negativity that lurks around seeking entrance to my mind is eliminated and I am refreshed looking around at the benefits the universe has allowed.

The dark places in my life have caused me to be grateful. In 2003 and 2009, I had serious health scares that threw me into a whirlwind of depression. I was angry that I was chosen to bear the scars of diabetes and heart disease in the prime of my life. There was no more fun for me. A dark and foreboding spirit became my best friend day and night. I focused on what was wrong with me instead of being grateful for the fact that I was still alive. My spiritual guide, who was also my husband, patiently worked with me and encouraged me daily to look at the positive side of things and the other good treasures that life has to offer. Grateful is what I am that this strong spirit was in my life at that low point. Grateful that he carried my burden when I almost gave up. I am forever indebted to the Universe that I found gratefulness in the dark.

You're not as bad off as you think you are. There are others in worse situations than what you are facing right now. Take a pen and pad and begin to write down what is right in your life. The people that have made a positive impact on you; focus on those things. Take out time to say how grateful and appreciative you are for those people and things, loud it to the universe, and watch your situation and mind shift to another level of gratefulness and positive energy.

GRATEFUL EVERYDAY

Colossians 3:15 | KJV

And let the peace of God rule in your hearts, to the which also ye are called in one body; and be ye thankful.

GRATEFUL EVERYDAY

NOTE

GRATEFUL EVERYDAY

NOTE

_____
_____
_____
_____
_____
_____
_____
_____
_____
_____
_____
_____
_____
_____
_____
_____

GRATEFUL EVERYDAY

NOTE

_____
_____
_____
_____
_____
_____
_____
_____
_____
_____
_____
_____
_____
_____
_____
_____
_____
_____

GRATEFUL EVERYDAY

NOTE

_____
_____
_____
_____
_____
_____
_____
_____
_____
_____
_____
_____
_____
_____
_____
_____
_____
_____

GRATEFUL EVERYDAY

NOTE

_____
_____
_____
_____
_____
_____
_____
_____
_____
_____
_____
_____
_____
_____
_____
_____

GRATEFUL EVERYDAY

NOTE

_____
_____
_____
_____
_____
_____
_____
_____
_____
_____
_____
_____
_____
_____
_____
_____

GRATEFUL EVERYDAY

NOTE

_____

_____

_____

_____

_____

_____

_____

_____

_____

_____

_____

_____

_____

_____

_____

_____

_____

_____

GRATEFUL EVERYDAY

NOTE

_____
_____
_____
_____
_____
_____
_____
_____
_____
_____
_____
_____
_____
_____
_____
_____
_____
_____

GRATEFUL EVERYDAY

NOTE

_____
_____
_____
_____
_____
_____
_____
_____
_____
_____
_____
_____
_____
_____
_____
_____

GRATEFUL EVERYDAY

NOTE

_____
_____
_____
_____
_____
_____
_____
_____
_____
_____
_____
_____
_____
_____
_____
_____
_____

GRATEFUL EVERYDAY

NOTE

GRATEFUL EVERYDAY

NOTE

GRATEFUL EVERYDAY

NOTE

_____
_____
_____
_____
_____
_____
_____
_____
_____
_____
_____
_____
_____
_____
_____
_____

GRATEFUL EVERYDAY

NOTE

_____
_____
_____
_____
_____
_____
_____
_____
_____
_____
_____
_____
_____
_____
_____

GRATEFUL EVERYDAY

NOTE

_____
_____
_____
_____
_____
_____
_____
_____
_____
_____
_____
_____
_____
_____
_____
_____
_____
_____

GRATEFUL EVERYDAY

NOTE

_____
_____
_____
_____
_____
_____
_____
_____
_____
_____
_____
_____
_____
_____
_____
_____
_____
_____

GRATEFUL EVERYDAY

NOTE

_____
_____
_____
_____
_____
_____
_____
_____
_____
_____
_____
_____
_____
_____
_____
_____
_____

GRATEFUL EVERYDAY

NOTE

_____
_____
_____
_____
_____
_____
_____
_____
_____
_____
_____
_____
_____
_____
_____
_____
_____